KINGDOM
GOVERNMENT

GOD'S DIVINE ORDER FOR BUILDING
HIS FAMILY ON EARTH

TOM CORNELL

KINGDOM GOVERNMENT

GOD'S DIVINE ORDER FOR BUILDING HIS FAMILY ON EARTH

TOM CORNELL

SOZO PUBLISHING

CONTENTS

INTRODUCTION
WHY CHURCH GOVERNMENT MATTERS

When people hear the word "government," especially in the church, they often think of control, politics, or hierarchy. But in God's house, government doesn't begin with control—it begins with care. It's not about who gets to be in charge; it's about how the Father protects, provides, and nurtures His family through divine order.

The truth is, God is a God of government. Before there was sin, before there was Israel, and before there was even a church—there was government in Heaven. God's throne, His angelic hosts, His decrees, His dominion—it all operated in perfect alignment.

When God created the world, He established order in creation. When He created family, He built it on headship, honor, and mutual submission. And when He birthed the Church, His eternal plan was to govern it, not from the top down, but from the inside out—with His Son as the Head, and His Spirit dwelling in every member.

Yet in our generation, many believers have only seen two

extremes: either abusive authority that wounds and controls, or absent authority that leaves people uncovered and unsafe. But there is a better way. There is a Kingdom way. And it's not man-made—it's revealed by the Spirit and rooted in Scripture.

The goal of this book is simple but significant: To help you understand how God governs His Church. Not through man's wisdom, but through the biblical blueprint of apostles, prophets, elders, deacons, bishops, and Spirit-led structure.

This isn't a book just for pastors or church leaders—it's for every believer who wants to understand how the Father builds His house, why leadership matters, and how healthy government actually releases growth, protection, and maturity in the body of Christ.

God's Government Is Not About Control—It's About Care

When a child is raised in a healthy family, they feel safe. They may not understand every rule, but they know they are loved. They grow, they flourish, and eventually they mature enough to carry the family name and even raise families of their own.

This is the same spirit of healthy church government. It's not about keeping people in line—it's about helping sons and daughters grow strong under the care of spiritual fathers and mothers who carry the Father's heart.

True spiritual authority always flows from love, humility, and alignment with the Head—Jesus Christ. And any structure or leader that operates outside of that—no matter how gifted—is operating outside the heart of God.

Why This Book Is Needed

You may be asking:

- Why do churches need elders, deacons, or bishops?
- Why can't we all just follow Jesus with no titles or structure?
- What's the difference between a pastor and an apostle?
- Isn't all this man-made hierarchy?

These are fair questions. In fact, many people have walked away from the church entirely because of misuse or misunderstanding of authority. Others have grown up in churches that had no biblical order at all—just democratic votes, power struggles, or no real oversight.

But when you open the New Testament, you don't find confusion. You find clarity. You see that from the very beginning, Jesus built His Church with structure: apostles to lay foundations, elders to shepherd, deacons to serve, bishops to oversee, and the fivefold ministry to equip the saints for works of service.

You see that the early Church grew, thrived, and endured persecution because of the strength of its government—not in spite of it.

God Builds According to a Pattern

In the Old Testament, when Moses was told to build the tabernacle, God said:

"See that you make everything according to the pattern shown you on the mountain." – Hebrews 8:5 NIV

This was not just about furniture—it was about function. God gave blueprints for a reason: because glory rests on what is built according to His pattern. The same is true for the Church today.

We don't get to make it up as we go. We are not called to vote on God's design. We are called to discern it, honor it, and align with it. When we build with His blueprint, the glory comes. The presence of God fills the house. The people grow strong. And the Kingdom expands.

Church Is a Family, Not a Business

Throughout this book, you'll hear this phrase repeated: The church is a family, not a business. That means we don't lead like CEOs, vote like shareholders, or perform like employees. We are sons and daughters, fathers and mothers, brothers and sisters.

Every role in the house exists to serve the well-being of the whole body. Just as healthy families have roles—parents who guide, children who grow, elders who bring wisdom—so does God's house. And when those roles are honored, the household flourishes.

What This Book Will Cover

Here's what you can expect in the chapters ahead:

- You'll learn about God's original design for government, not just in theory, but in practice.
- You'll discover how Jesus governs His Church through fivefold ministry, elders, deacons, and bishops.
- You'll see how spiritual covering, submission, and accountability are actually life-giving and freeing.
- You'll understand what makes government healthy or unhealthy, and how to discern the difference.

- You'll gain vision for the Church as a Kingdom force, not just a Sunday gathering.

Whether you are new to these ideas or you've been in church your whole life, this book is meant to give you clarity, confidence, and conviction about what you're a part of—and how you can walk in alignment with Heaven's pattern.

The End Goal: Christ the Head, His Body in Order

When Jesus said, "I will build My Church, and the gates of hell will not prevail against it" (Matthew 16:18), He wasn't speaking about a loose collection of individuals. He was speaking about a governed, aligned, Spirit-filled people who know how to follow, how to lead, and how to stand strong together.

The world is full of chaos. The enemy thrives on disorder. But God's glory rests on what is in order. That's why this matters. So whether you're reading this as a new believer, a growing disciple, or a member wanting to understand your place in the family—know this: You were never meant to be alone. You were meant to be part of a house—built by the Spirit, governed by love, and filled with glory. Let's learn together how that house is built.

1

THE GOVERNMENT OF GOD
HEAVENS PATTERN ON EARTH

Most people don't associate the word "government" with comfort or safety. In our world, government often stirs thoughts of control, politics, or red tape. But when we talk about the government of God, we're talking about something holy, pure, and beautiful. We're talking about how a loving Father brings order to His family so His people can thrive.

Before there was ever a church, a nation, or a family, there was God—and He ruled in perfect peace. He didn't rule because anyone voted for Him. He ruled because He is the source of life, wisdom, and righteousness. And from the very beginning, God's way of doing things—His government—has always reflected His character: just, merciful, wise, and good.

The Kingdom Is a Government, Not a Democracy

Isaiah prophesied of Jesus:

"For to us a child is born, to us a son is given; and the government will be on his shoulders... Of the increase of his government and peace there will be no end." – Isaiah 9:6–7 NIV

Notice what's being described: not just the birth of a Savior, but the arrival of a government. Jesus didn't come to start a religion. He came to reestablish the Kingdom of Heaven on Earth, to reclaim what Adam lost, and to bring humanity back under God's rule.

His Kingdom is not built on votes, popularity, or compromise. It's built on truth, love, righteousness, and order.That means the Church—His Body on Earth—is not a democracy. We don't get to decide what's true, what leadership should look like, or how to build. We are stewards of a heavenly pattern. Jesus is the King, and He governs through delegated authority and divine order.

Jesus Is the Head, and We Are His Body

Ephesians 1:22–23 tells us:

"And He put all things [in every realm] in subjection under Christ's feet, and appointed Him as supreme and authoritative head over all things in the church, which is His body, the fullness of Him who fills and completes all things in all believers." AMP

Jesus is not just Savior and Friend. He is the Head. That means He directs, leads, orders, and builds. And just like a physical body only functions when the head is in charge, the Church only flourishes when it submits to the leadership of Christ.

But here's the key: Christ expresses His headship through people. He speaks to His Body through His Word and by His Spirit—but He also leads through servant- hearted leadership, through spiritual mothers and fathers, and through biblical roles like apostles, elders, and deacons.

When the Body is rightly connected to the Head—honoring

His Word, obeying His Spirit, and respecting His design—the whole Church becomes healthy, growing, and full of life.

God Always Governs Through Order

From Genesis to Revelation, one thing is clear: God moves where there is order.

- In Genesis 1, the Spirit hovered over the chaos—but creation didn't happen until God spoke order into it.
- In Exodus, the glory of God didn't fall on the tabernacle until Moses built it according to the heavenly pattern.
- In the early Church, the outpouring of the Holy Spirit in Acts 2 was followed by apostolic leadership and daily order (Acts 2:42–47).
- Even in Heaven, we see thrones, elders, angels, and roles of authority all working in perfect alignment.

God's nature is not chaotic. He brings peace by bringing structure. Where there is divine order, there is divine presence. That's why God governs His Church. Not to limit us—but to free us to flourish. Not to control us—but to cover us. Not to silence us—but to synchronize us with Heaven's rhythm.

God's Government Is a Family Model

One of the biggest misconceptions is that God's government is cold or institutional. But the truth is, God's government is deeply relational. It flows from the heart of a Father, and it's expressed through a family. That means the Church is not run like a corporation. It's led like a household.

Just as a family has parents, children, roles, and rhythms, so does God's house. In 1 Timothy 3, Paul makes the point that leaders in the church must first know how to lead their own homes—because church leadership is simply an extension of family leadership.

God's government is not about climbing ladders. It's about carrying responsibility for others. True authority in the Church is not earned by ambition, but entrusted through maturity. Those who lead are not bosses—they are builders, guardians, and servants of God's people.

The Fruit of Divine Government

When God's government is honored, the results speak for themselves:

- Clarity replaces confusion.
- Unity replaces division.
- Growth replaces stagnation.
- Protection replaces vulnerability.
- Multiplication replaces control.

Psalm 133 says that where there is unity, God commands the blessing. But unity doesn't come through wishful thinking—it comes through alignment. And alignment only happens when people willingly come under God's pattern.

Think about a flock of sheep. They need a shepherd. Not because they're weak, but because their strength is in their togetherness. When a shepherd leads with love, the flock finds safety, food, rest, and direction. That's how God designed His people to thrive—not isolated, but covered; not scattered, but ordered.

Why This Matters to You

You may not see yourself as a leader. You may think this is

something for pastors or elders to worry about. But the truth is, you are part of a divine construction project.

Ephesians 2:19–22 says:

"You are... members of God's household, built on the foundation of the apostles and prophets, with Christ Jesus himself as the chief cornerstone. In him the whole building is joined together and rises to become a holy temple in the Lord." NIV

You are part of the house. And if you're part of the house, you need to know how it's built. This chapter is not just a lesson in church structure. It's an invitation to see God's heart as a Builder, a Father, and a King. He builds with wisdom. He builds with purpose. And most importantly, He builds with you in mind.

In Summary

- God's Kingdom is a government, not a democracy.
- Jesus is the Head of the Church, and He governs through order, not confusion.
- God's government is not about control—it's about care, protection, and purpose.
- Healthy government creates room for growth, multiplication, and maturity.
- You are not just a bystander—you're a living stone in God's house, and understanding His government helps you find your place in the family.

Activation Prayer

Father, I thank You that Your Kingdom is not chaos but peace, not confusion but order, not control but care. I acknowledge today that Jesus is the Head of the Church and the King of my life. I willingly come under Your government—Your truth, Your love, and Your wisdom. Lord, align my heart with Heaven's pattern. Where I've resisted authority, bring humility. Where I've feared control, show me Your Fatherly care. Where I've lived scattered, connect me to Your family. I declare that I am a living stone in Your house. Build me into Your holy temple. Teach me to honor the leaders and brothers and sisters You've placed around me. Make me a vessel of unity, growth, and protection in Your Body. Holy Spirit, fill me with grace to walk in alignment. Let my life carry the order of Heaven so that Your presence can dwell in me and through me. I receive my place in Your divine design. In Jesus' name, Amen.

Discussion Questions

1 . Isaiah 9 says the government will be on Jesus' shoulders. How does seeing the Kingdom as a *government under a King*(rather than a democracy) challenge the way you think about truth, leadership, and your role in the Church?

2 . The chapter highlights that God moves where there is order —from creation, to the tabernacle, to the early church. Where do you see the need for greater order in your own life or community, and how might bringing things into alignment with God's pattern invite His presence?

3 . God's government flows like a family, not a corporation. How does this picture of servant-hearted, relational leadership change your expectations of leaders—and your own part as a "living stone" in God's house?

2

FIVEFOLD MINISTRY
CHRIST'S GIFTS FOR GOVERNMENT AND GROWTH

When Jesus rose from the dead, He didn't just forgive our sins and conquer the grave—He also gave gifts to His people. These weren't material gifts. They weren't rewards for good behavior. These were leadership gifts—people given to people—so that the Church could grow strong, stay healthy, and reflect Christ in every area of life.

Ephesians 4:11–13 says:

"So Christ himself gave the apostles, the prophets, the evangelists, the pastors and teachers, to equip his people for works of service, so that the body of Christ may be built up until we all reach unity in the faith and in the knowledge of the Son of God and become mature, attaining to the whole measure of the fullness of Christ."
NIV

This passage is often referred to as the fivefold ministry. But before we break down these roles, it's important to understand why they matter—not just to leaders, but to every believer. These gifts are not a hierarchy to climb. They are a blueprint to build with. They don't exist so people can have titles—they exist to train, equip, and empower the saints to become like Jesus and carry His Kingdom into every part of the Earth.

Christ Gave Gifts — Not Just to the Church, But for the Church

The fivefold ministry is not man's idea. It's Christ's idea. The Bible says "He Himself gave..." That means these roles carry divine authority and intentionality. They were given to produce something specific: a mature Church, full of unity, full of love, and full of Christ's nature. If we ignore these gifts, we stay immature.

If we reduce the Church to just one or two gifts—like only pastors or only teachers—we become imbalanced and ineffective. But when all five gifts are honored and functioning, the Church becomes strong, healthy, and fruitful.

The Five Gifts of Christ

Let's look briefly at each of these gifts and what they contribute to the life of the Church.

1. Apostles — The Architects and Fathers

Apostles are sent ones. They are pioneers, planters, and builders. But more than that, they carry a fathering spirit. Apostles don't just lead movements—they raise sons and daughters. They don't just build churches—they establish culture, set order, and lay strong foundations.

In Scripture, apostles governed regions, appointed elders, solved disputes, and ensured that churches were aligned with Christ's teaching. Their job wasn't to control, but to anchor the Church to Christ as the foundation.

Apostles carry vision, governmental grace, and the ability to father a family of churches or ministries. Without them, the Church often becomes disconnected, shallow, or stuck in survival mode.

2. Prophets — The Voice of Heaven

Prophets hear God's heart and declare His Word. They see what others don't and call the Church back to its true purpose. Prophets don't just predict the future—they reveal God's current desire, correct drift, and stir the Body toward holiness and passion.

Prophets help the Church stay spiritually sensitive and responsive. They help leaders hear what Heaven is saying and ensure the Church doesn't become religious, cold, or political. When prophets are functioning rightly, they equip others to hear God, not just depend on them.

3. Evangelists — The Gatherers and Fire-Starters

Evangelists are soul-winners. They carry a burden for the lost and the ability to communicate the Gospel in a way that awakens hearts. But they also equip the Church to share Jesus boldly—not just to preach in church, but to live on mission every day.

Evangelists stir urgency, compassion, and joy. They remind the Church that we were saved to share, not to sit. Their fire keeps the Church alive with passion and outward focus.

4. Pastors — The Shepherds of the Flock

Pastors love the people. They comfort, guide, and walk with the sheep through life's valleys and mountaintops. They don't just teach truth—they walk it out with others, bearing burdens and cultivating community.

Pastors guard the flock from wolves, protect unity, and help people feel safe and known. But pastors are not the entire Church structure. When they work alongside the other gifts, especially apostles and teachers, they can shepherd without carrying everything alone.

5. Teachers — The Builders of Understanding

Teachers ground the Church in truth. They help people understand Scripture and apply it. Teachers take what's deep and make it clear. They don't just give information—they cultivate transformation. Without teaching, the Church becomes emotional but unstable. With good teaching, the foundation of faith is strong, the mind is renewed, and false doctrine is exposed and corrected.

Five Gifts, One Purpose: Equipping the Saints

The goal of all five gifts is not personal platforms—it's people. The gifts exist to equip the saints for the work of ministry. Every believer is called to carry the Gospel, demonstrate the Kingdom, and reflect Christ. But it takes equipping to do that. That's why these gifts must be received—not just respected.

When leaders function in their grace and equip others, the Body becomes mature and effective. This means the fivefold ministry is not a stage to watch, but a family to be trained by. These gifts are meant to give away their grace—to raise people up into maturity, boldness, and purpose.

Apostolic Leadership: The Fathering Gift

Among the five, the apostolic gift often functions as a governing grace. Not in dominance, but in fatherhood. Apostolic leaders are not better than the others. But they often have the blueprint, the long-term vision, and the ability to set things in order.

They see the house, not just the room. They think generationally, not just organizationally. And most of all, they raise sons and daughters who carry the spirit of the house.When apostles are present, church government becomes aligned, secure, and fruitful.

They work with prophets to hear from God, with evangelists to stir the mission, with pastors to love the people, and with teachers to ground the truth. In many ways, they father the other gifts and ensure the whole family is thriving.

Why This Matters to You

You may not be called to be one of the fivefold gifts, but you are absolutely called to be equipped by them. If you're in Christ, you are a saint—and you have a calling, a purpose, and a role in God's plan.

The fivefold ministry helps you:

- Grow in spiritual maturity
- Discover your gifts and calling
- Be healed, restored, and sent
- Learn how to carry the culture of Heaven in your world

And as you grow, you'll find yourself mirroring some of these gifts. Many believers reflect apostolic vision, prophetic insight, pastoral care, evangelistic passion, or teaching clarity—even if they're not holding an office. That's because these gifts don't just live on a platform. They live in the Body.

In Summary

- Jesus gave apostles, prophets, evangelists, pastors, and teachers to equip His people.
- Each gift plays a vital role in maturing the Church and reflecting Christ fully.
- The apostolic gift helps govern, father, and align the Church to Heaven's blueprint.
- You are called to be equipped—and these gifts exist to help you become like Jesus and live on mission.

Activation Prayer

Jesus, thank You that when You rose from the grave, You didn't just defeat sin and death—you gave gifts to Your people so that we could grow into Your likeness. I honor the gifts You've given: apostles, prophets, evangelists, pastors, and teachers. I choose to receive their grace and allow their ministry to equip me for the work of serving others and carrying Your Kingdom. Lord, mature me through Your gifts. Heal what is broken, train me where I am unprepared, and release me into the fullness of the calling You've placed on my life. Teach me to carry the culture of Heaven into my family, workplace, and community. Holy Spirit, show me which of these graces You are stirring in me to reflect—whether apostolic vision, prophetic clarity, evangelistic fire, pastoral care, or teaching truth. I surrender myself to Your design, and I say: build me, equip me, and send me. In Jesus' name, Amen.

Discussion Questions

1 . Ephesians 4 says Christ Himself gave the fivefold gifts to
His Church. Why is it important to see these leaders as *gifts
from Jesus*, and how does that shift the way we relate to spiritual
leadership?

2 . The chapter warns that if we only function in one or two
gifts (like pastors or teachers), the Church becomes imbalanced. In what ways have you seen the Body become stronger
when all five gifts are working together?

3 . These gifts exist to equip *you* for ministry. Which of the five
areas (apostolic, prophetic, evangelistic, pastoral, teaching)
do you sense God wants to strengthen in your life right now?
How can you actively receive that equipping?

3

ELDERS

SHEPHERDS OF THE FLOCK

E very healthy family has mature parents. Not perfect ones, but wise, present, and trustworthy ones who love the children and carry the heart of the Father. In the same way, God's house—the Church—has elders, who are mature spiritual leaders tasked with shepherding the people, teaching sound doctrine, and making decisions that protect and build the Body.

When the New Testament speaks of church leadership, the role of "elder" appears repeatedly, and always in the context of plurality, maturity, and responsibility. Elders are not the elite— they are servants who lead through character, wisdom, and spiritual authority. They don't just have a title—they carry a burden.

Who Are Elders?

In Scripture, the word "elder" (Greek: presbyteros) means "older" or "mature one." But it doesn't refer only to age—it points to spiritual maturity, tested character, and proven love for God and His people. Elders are not chosen because of popularity or charisma.

They're recognized because of who they already are in the community: faithful, trustworthy, wise, and wholehearted. They are men (and at times women, depending on church conviction) who have walked with God, served quietly, endured trials, and demonstrated leadership through example before position.

The Bible describes their qualifications in places like 1 Timothy 3 and Titus 1. These passages emphasize character over skill: faithfulness to one's spouse, sober-mindedness, hospitality, gentleness, sound doctrine, and integrity.Elders are the kind of people you can trust with your soul, not just with your schedule.

What Do Elders Do?

Elders carry both spiritual and practical authority. They do the work of shepherds—caring for people's hearts, protecting from deception, correcting in love, and guiding the flock through seasons of growth and change. Here are some of the key roles elders fulfill:

1. Shepherding the Flock

Elders are called to "shepherd the flock of God among you" (1 Peter 5:2). This means they care for the people—not in a controlling way, but in a fatherly, watchful way. They pray for the sick, counsel the hurting, guide the young, and make sure no sheep gets lost in the shuffle. Their leadership is not distant—it's relational. They know the people, walk among them, and serve as trusted voices in their lives.

2. Teaching Sound Doctrine

Paul told Titus that elders must "hold firm to the trustworthy word... so that he may be able to give instruction in sound doctrine and also to rebuke those who contradict it" (Titus 1:9).

In other words, elders are guardians of truth. They don't need to be eloquent preachers, but they must be able to teach the truth faithfully, live it with integrity, and confront error when needed. In a world full of compromise, elders help anchor the Church to the Word of God.

3. Overseeing and Making Decisions

Elders are also responsible for governing the local church. They make decisions about direction, discipline, doctrine, and delegation. This doesn't mean they act like a corporate board-room—far from it. Their decisions are made prayerfully, as shepherds discerning the will of God together.

Their goal is never control—it's always the health and fruitfulness of the Body. They exist to preserve unity, protect the sheep, and pursue the will of God for the local church family.

Plural Leadership, Shared Authority

One of the clearest patterns in the New Testament is that elders are always plural. There's no example of a single elder running the whole church. Instead, we see teams of elders leading together under the headship of Christ.

This is important. No one man (or woman) has it all. Shared leadership brings balance, safety, and wisdom. Where one elder may have strong teaching, another may have great discernment. Where one is bold, another is pastoral. Together, they reflect the fullness of Christ's care.

Elder teams are not democratic, where votes decide everything. Nor are they hierarchical, where one elder dominates. They are spiritual families, led by the Spirit, often with a lead elder or house pastor who facilitates but does not dominate.

Elders Under Apostolic Covering

Though elders oversee the local church, they are not isolated or autonomous. In the early Church, elders functioned under apostolic covering. Apostles planted churches, appointed elders, and returned to strengthen them.

This doesn't make elders less authoritative—it makes them accountable and aligned. Just as every family needs both parents and grandparents, every local church needs elders who are under spiritual covering, not operating independently.

Apostolic leadership helps elders stay aligned with the broader Kingdom mission, receive correction when needed, and avoid stagnation or internal politics. Elders function best when they are both submitted and secure.

Elders Are Shepherds, Not Lords

Peter gave elders a clear warning:

"Shepherd the flock of God... not domineering over those in your charge, but being examples to the flock." – 1 Peter 5:2–3 ESV

The spirit of eldership is not pride—it's fatherhood. Elders are called to serve, not rule; to carry, not crush. Their leadership flows from love, not fear. They don't need titles to have authority—their lives are the message. Jesus said, "The greatest among you will be your servant."

Elders lead by getting low, not by climbing high. They are willing to stay up late, show up early, and walk slowly with people through pain and process. They reflect the heart of the Good Shepherd.

Elders and the People

As a member of a church, you should know your elders. You should pray for them, honor them, and go to them when you need guidance. They are not distant authorities, but present fathers and mothers in the house.

Hebrews 13:17 says:

> *"Obey your leaders and submit to them, for they are keeping watch over your souls, as those who will have to give an account." ESV*

That's a heavy responsibility. And it means that when you follow godly elders, you're not giving up freedom—you're gaining protection. You don't have to agree with every decision, but you should honor the office and posture your heart with trust. In doing so, you help build a house where God's presence and peace dwell richly.

In Summary

- Elders are mature spiritual leaders appointed to shepherd the local church.
- They teach, govern, care for people, and guard the truth.
- They lead as a team under the covering of apostolic leadership.
- Their authority is rooted in love, not control.
- When elders lead well and people follow with honor, the church becomes a safe and fruitful family.

. . .

Activation Prayer

Father, I thank You for the gift of elders in Your house. Thank You for wise, mature leaders who carry Your heart, teach Your Word, and shepherd Your people. I pray for those You've placed in leadership over me—strengthen them, protect them, and fill them with wisdom and love. Lord, help me to honor spiritual authority rightly, not with fear but with trust. Teach me to see elders as shepherds, not lords; as servants, not rulers. Where my heart has resisted authority, soften me. Where I have been critical, give me a spirit of prayer and encouragement. Holy Spirit, continue to grow me into maturity so that I can also be a faithful steward in Your house—whether as an elder one day or as a trusted son or daughter who supports the leaders You've given. May my life help build a safe, fruitful, and Spirit-filled family where Your presence dwells. In Jesus' name, Amen.

Discussion Questions

1 . This chapter emphasizes that elders are recognized for their maturity and character, not just appointed for their skill or charisma. Why do you think God values character more than gifting when it comes to leadership?

2 . The New Testament shows that elders always led in teams. How does shared leadership protect a church from imbalance, and how can we cultivate that same spirit of shared responsibility in our families, teams, or small groups?

3 . Hebrews 13:17 says elders keep watch over our souls. How can we, as members of a local church, support, honor, and pray for our leaders so they can lead with joy instead of weariness?

4

DEACONS
SERVANTS WHO LEAD THROUGH ACTION

E very house needs people who serve with faithfulness, joy, and initiative. In the natural, these are the ones who clean, organize, troubleshoot, and help things run smoothly behind the scenes. In God's house, we call them deacons—and their role is both practical and spiritual, humble and honorable.

While elders focus on spiritual oversight, deacons free them to do that by handling the practical needs of the church. But don't mistake their behind-the-scenes nature for a lesser calling. Deacons are vital to the life of the church. In fact, they were the first ministry team appointed in the Book of Acts—and they were chosen because of their maturity and integrity. Deacons teach us that real leadership doesn't begin with a microphone—it begins with a towel.

Who Are Deacons?

The word "deacon" comes from the Greek word "diakonos", which means servant, helper, or minister. While every believer is called to serve, the New Testament makes a distinction for those who are recognized as official deacons—those set apart for consistent, trusted service in God's house. The first deacons were appointed in Acts 6. As the church grew, some widows were being overlooked in the daily distribution of food. The apostles said:

"It is not right that we should give up preaching the word of God to serve tables. Therefore, brothers, pick out from among you seven men of good repute, full of the Spirit and of wisdom, whom we will appoint to this duty." – Acts 6:2–3 ESV

This wasn't about elevating one type of service over another. It was about assigning each person to their God-given role so the church could grow without confusion or burnout. The apostles knew they were called to spiritual oversight and the Word. So, they empowered deacons to take leadership over practical needs— not just to do tasks, but to carry a burden with excellence and care.

The Qualifications of a Deacon

Deacons are not just hard workers—they are godly, trustworthy, Spirit-filled believers. Their character is the foundation of their ministry. Paul outlines their qualifications in 1 Timothy 3:8–13. Let's look at a few key qualities:

- Dignified: They carry themselves with honor, integrity, and maturity.
- Not double-tongued: They speak truthfully, not gossiping or manipulating.
- Not greedy for dishonest gain: They steward resources with purity and accountability.
- Holding the mystery of the faith with a clear conscience: They understand the gospel and live it.
- Tested: They have already shown faithfulness before being recognized.

Paul also mentions the importance of their households—how they relate to their spouse and children. Why? Because the way someone leads at home reveals how they will lead in the house of God. Faithful deacons are often hidden heroes.

They may not have a public platform, but they're the first to show up, the last to leave, and the ones who carry weight others don't even see. And according to Paul, those who serve well "gain a good standing and great confidence in the faith" (1 Tim. 3:13).

What Do Deacons Do?

Deacons handle natural affairs with spiritual excellence. Here are some examples of the kinds of tasks deacons may oversee:

- Facility care and hospitality
- Finances, counting offerings, stewarding resources
- Organizing events, meals, or outreach logistics
- Serving communion or water baptisms
- Coordinating teams for parking, security, or welcome ministry
- Caring for widows, practical needs, or benevolence
- Administrative support for leaders and ministries

In short, they serve where there's a need and build where there's a gap. But again, this is not just busywork. These tasks are spiritual offerings. They create an atmosphere where others can encounter God, hear His Word, and receive ministry without distraction or disorder.

Their Relationship to Elders

Deacons don't exist to replace elders or to compete with them —they exist to complement and support them. While elders carry the responsibility for spiritual leadership, deacons handle the practical demands that could otherwise become distractions or burdens to the elders. When this dynamic works correctly, it creates a beautiful rhythm:

- Elders lead by vision, prayer, teaching, and shepherding.
- Deacons lead by action, service, support, and follow-through.

This allows elders to stay in the Word and prayer (Acts 6:4) while knowing that the operations and natural affairs of the church are being carried out with excellence. It also gives the congregation a clear model to follow—honoring both spiritual and practical gifts in the house. A healthy local church needs both the wisdom of elders and the faithfulness of deacons.

Deacons as Ministers, Not Just Workers

It's important to remember: deacons are ministers. They may not preach from a pulpit, but they minister through presence, responsibility, and example. One of the first deacons appointed in Acts 6 was Stephen. And what do we see him doing in the next chapter? Preaching with power, working miracles, and standing boldly for Jesus—even to the point of martyrdom.

Another deacon, Philip, becomes an evangelist who preaches to cities and leads an Ethiopian eunuch to salvation and baptism. Clearly, being a deacon is not a "less than" role—it's a Kingdom launchpad. Serving well in practical things often leads to open doors in spiritual things. Why?

Because God tests our hearts with small things before trusting us with greater ones. Jesus said, "The greatest among you will be your servant."

Deacons and the People

If you're a member of a church, you've probably been blessed by a deacon even if you didn't realize it. They're the ones making sure the building is clean, the chairs are straight, the events run smoothly, and people are cared for when they're in need.

But more than that, they are models of love and consistency. They show up when others don't. They give without expecting recognition. They reflect the heart of Jesus, who "did not come to be served, but to serve." Honor the deacons among you. Don't overlook their role. They help build the atmosphere of a house that welcomes the Spirit and invites transformation.

In Summary

- Deacons are servant-leaders who handle the practical needs of the church.
- Their qualifications are spiritual: proven character, faith, and integrity.
- They work closely with elders, freeing them to focus on spiritual matters.
- Their work is not lesser—it is powerful, essential, and often supernatural.
- Faithful deacons open doors for greater ministry through their service.

. . .

Activation Prayer

Jesus, thank You for modeling servant leadership and showing us that true greatness is found in humility and service. I thank You for the deacons in Your house—those who serve faithfully, joyfully, and often unseen. Bless them, strengthen them, and reward them openly for what they carry in secret. Lord, teach me to see every act of service as a holy offering. Whether I'm cleaning, organizing, giving, or supporting others, let me do it with excellence and love. Shape my heart to serve without recognition, to carry responsibility with joy, and to reflect Your servant-hearted nature in all I do. Holy Spirit, help me to embrace the call to be faithful in the small things so You can trust me with greater things. May my life carry the fragrance of Christ's humility, and may my service create space for others to encounter You. In Jesus' name, Amen.

Discussion Questions

1. This chapter says, *"Real leadership doesn't begin with a microphone—it begins with a towel."* How does this statement challenge cultural ideas of leadership, and what does it reveal about Jesus' model of greatness?

2. The qualifications of deacons (1 Tim. 3:8–13) focus on integrity, faith, and maturity rather than skill or visibility. Why do you think God emphasizes character so strongly in those who serve?

3. The chapter shows that deacons like Stephen and Philip didn't stay hidden—they stepped into powerful ministry. How can serving in practical ways today prepare us for greater opportunities in Kingdom ministry tomorrow?

5

BISHOPS
OVERSEERS OF OVERSIGHT

I f elders are shepherds of a local flock and deacons are servants of practical need, then bishops are those who oversee the overseers. In many ways, bishops carry the heart of a spiritual parent—not just for one local church, but often for a region, a network, or multiple congregations.

They provide stability, alignment, and apostolic care to leaders who are caring for others. To understand bishops, we must first clear up confusion that has come from centuries of church history.

The word "bishop" has been used in many traditions to mean different things—sometimes a ceremonial role, sometimes a political one. But if we return to the Scriptures and let the Word define the role, we'll see something powerful: bishops are not distant officials—they are fathers in the faith.

What Does the Bible Say About Bishops?

The Greek word translated bishop in the New Testament is "episkopos", meaning overseer or one who watches over. This word is used interchangeably in Scripture with the terms for elder (presbyteros) and shepherd (poimen), especially in reference to the local church. For example:

"...if anyone aspires to the office of overseer (episkope), he desires a noble task." — 1 Timothy 3:1 ESV

"Pay careful attention to yourselves and to all the flock, in which the Holy Spirit has made you overseers (episkopos), to care for the church of God..." — Acts 20:28 ESV

This shows that in the early church, the role of bishop was not a separate hierarchy above elders—it was often a functional title for someone doing oversight. However, as churches multiplied and matured, some overseers began to carry responsibility over multiple churches or groups of elders.

This is where the modern understanding of bishop begins to take shape. A bishop is not someone with a fancy title—it is someone who carries spiritual weight and watches over other leaders with wisdom, love, and authority.

The Role of the Bishop: Oversight and Maturity

While all elders have oversight of their own local church, a bishop has a broader assignment. They may oversee:

- Multiple churches in a city or region
- A network of pastors and elders
- A training center or apostolic hub
- A family of ministries, leaders, or house churches

Bishops are not just administrating—they are governing through relationship, presence, and fatherhood. They provide:

- Doctrinal alignment to guard against false teaching or drifting theology
- Relational unity between leaders and churches
- Correction and counsel when a local elder is in need• Spiritual protection and intercession for the churches under their care

In essence, a bishop is like a spiritual parent to leaders who themselves are parenting churches. Their ministry brings consistency, correction, and covering.

What Kind of Person Becomes a Bishop?

Paul describes the qualifications for a bishop in 1 Timothy 3 and Titus 1, very similar to those of elders. Why? Because a bishop must first be an elder, tested and proven. There is no shortcut or promotion ladder. The office of bishop is simply a recognition of maturity, fathering capacity, and regional responsibility. Some marks of a bishop include:

- Proven fruit as an elder over time
- A life of integrity, hospitality, and spiritual discipline
- Sound doctrine and ability to teach
- A reputation of blamelessness in the eyes of outsiders
- A heart for the Body of Christ beyond just their local congregation
- The ability to handle correction, conflict, and restoration processes wisely

Bishops are not self-appointed—they are recognized by others for their grace and fruit. They are called by God, affirmed by the apostolic, and received by the churches.

Are Bishops Apostles?

This is a common question. The short answer: some are, but not all. And that distinction matters.

- A bishop is someone who oversees others, often within a known structure or network.
- An apostle is someone sent by Christ with authority to establish, pioneer, and govern according to divine blueprint.

There is significant overlap between the two roles, especially when a bishop moves in apostolic grace. In fact, many bishops function apostolically—training leaders, planting churches, imparting vision, and correcting doctrine. However, the term "apostle" carries a missionary, pioneering, and fathering mandate that goes beyond structure.

Every apostle may be a bishop in function. But not every bishop is an apostle in calling. The key is not the title, but the spiritual grace and responsibility carried. Jesus didn't give us titles —He gave us gifts (Ephesians 4:11). And we must honor people not by labels, but by fruit and function.

Why Bishops Matter in Today's Church

In today's rapidly expanding and often disconnected church world, the role of bishops is being restored—not as figureheads, but as wise overseers who protect the health of God's house. Without bishops:

- Churches can become isolated and unaccountable
- Elders may lack correction, care, or clarity in conflict
- Doctrinal drift becomes easier
- Regional disunity can hinder Kingdom advancement

With bishops:

- Churches are covered, connected, and strengthened
- Elders have fathers and mentors, not just peers
- Truth is guarded, and unity is preserved
- Apostolic vision can flow across territories

God is raising up a generation of bishops who don't just wear collars or carry titles—but who carry the Father's heart for the Body of Christ.

A Family of Families

Bishops remind us that the Church is not a business—it's a family. And just like in any healthy extended family, there are parents (elders), grandparents (bishops), and patriarchs (apostolic fathers) who help hold the generations together.

If you are part of a local church, your elders are your direct shepherds. But behind them, you may have a bishop—a mature overseer who helps guard the well-being of the house and the houses connected to it. That bishop is not your enemy or a distant boss. They are part of God's design for your protection, growth, and alignment.

When bishops walk in humility, wisdom, and spiritual authority, churches flourish. There is joy, peace, consistency, and fruit. And most importantly, Jesus remains the true head—with every joint supplying under His leadership.

In Summary

- Bishops (episkopos) are overseers who provide spiritual covering to elders and churches.
- Their role is deeply relational, rooted in maturity and proven leadership.

- Some bishops function as apostles, but not all apostles are bishops.
- Bishops bring unity, protection, correction, and connection across churches.
- They reflect the fathering heart of God for His growing family.

Activation Prayer

Father, thank You that You are a God of order, care, and covering. I honor the gift of bishops—those who watch over leaders and churches with the heart of a spiritual parent. Thank You for raising up overseers who carry maturity, wisdom, and the Father's love for Your family. Lord, I pray for the bishops in the Body of Christ today. Strengthen them with Your Spirit, protect them from weariness, and fill them with grace to father leaders and guard Your truth. Where the Church has misunderstood or misused titles, bring us back to the simplicity of function and fruit. Holy Spirit, teach me how to live under covering with honor, not suspicion. Align my heart with Your design so that I can walk in unity with the family of God. And help me grow in maturity so that my life also reflects faithfulness, integrity, and love for Your people. In Jesus' name, Amen.

Discussion Questions

1. . This chapter describes bishops as "fathers in the faith" who oversee leaders and churches. How does this perspective shift the way we think about authority—not as control, but as parental care?

2. . The teaching emphasizes that Jesus gave gifts, not titles (Eph. 4:11). Why is it dangerous to focus on labels like *bishop* or *apostle* instead of recognizing the fruit and function in someone's life?

3. . What are the risks of churches or leaders living without spiritual covering, and how can bishops help protect unity, truth, and accountability in the wider Body of Christ?

6

APOSTOLIC ORDER
LAYING THE FOUNDATION

When it comes to building anything that will last, the foundation is everything. You can have beautiful walls, innovative design, and vibrant paint—but if the foundation is cracked, unstable, or absent altogether, everything built on top of it is at risk. This is just as true in the Church.

Jesus Christ is the Chief Cornerstone—the unshakable center of the Church. But Scripture also tells us that the Church is "built on the foundation of the apostles and prophets, Christ Jesus Himself being the cornerstone" (Ephesians 2:20). That means apostolic and prophetic ministry are foundational, not optional. They don't replace Christ; they build upon Him with the blueprints of Heaven.

In this chapter, we'll explore how apostolic order is God's pattern for governing His Church, bringing strength, stability, and growth by laying the foundation of Christ rightly. Without it, churches often drift, divide, or become man-centered. But when apostles function properly—as fathers, builders, and vision-carriers—the Church becomes a powerful, unified body under Jesus' leadership.

Apostles as Master-Builders

Paul described himself this way:

"According to the grace of God given to me, like a skilled master builder I laid a foundation, and someone else is building upon it. Let each one take care how he builds upon it." — *1 Corinthians 3:10 ESV*

The Greek word Paul used for "master builder" is architekton —from which we get our word "architect." Apostles are spiritual architects. They don't just build emotional experiences or manage programs—they receive a blueprint from Heaven and build according to what God reveals.

Like Moses on the mountain, apostles receive the pattern and bring it down to the people. That's why apostles often show up when God is doing something new: planting churches, reforming structures, raising new leaders, or restoring biblical order.

They carry divine authority and a deep burden to see Christ formed in people and in the structure of the Church itself (Galatians 4:19). Without apostolic input, churches may still love Jesus—but they may lack form, alignment, and long-term strength.

Apostolic Authority Establishes and Corrects

Apostolic authority is not about control or dominance—it's about alignment and correction. Apostles bring churches and leaders into order, not just so things "run better," but so Christ can be revealed more fully. Here's what apostolic order does:

1. It brings clarity to the roles, callings, and functions of a church.

2. It aligns gifts and leadership into healthy flow—not competition, confusion, or chaos.
3. It corrects dysfunction—whether doctrinal error, spiritual immaturity, or relational breakdown.
4. It creates space for the other gifts (prophets, evangelists, pastors, teachers) to function properly.
5. It releases sons and daughters into maturity and ministry.

In Acts 15, when the early church faced a major doctrinal dispute about Gentiles and the Law, it was the apostles and elders who gathered in Jerusalem to bring clarity, correction, and alignment. That's apostolic order in action.

Apostolic government doesn't silence other voices—it harmonizes them. It doesn't dominate—it fathers. It doesn't replace the authority of Jesus—it makes His rule visible by helping the Church walk in truth and love.

Gifting vs. Governmental Grace

One of the greatest misunderstandings in the Church is assuming that spiritual gifting automatically means governmental authority. It doesn't. Many believers have powerful gifts: teaching, healing, prophecy, leadership, intercession, administration, and more. But a gift is not the same as a governing grace. For example:

- A person may be prophetic and deliver accurate words —but that does not make them a prophet who shapes doctrine, equips others, or carries spiritual authority.
- A person may be a great speaker or encourager—but that doesn't mean they are a pastor called to shepherd people long-term.
- Likewise, someone may start ministries or plant

churches, but if they are not submitted and proven, they may not carry true apostolic authority.

Gifts bless the Body. Government governs the Body. Gifts are for function. Governmental grace is for order.Apostolic grace is not just the ability to preach or plant churches—it is divine empowerment to father, govern, and align the Church to Christ's image and mission. It comes with great responsibility, humility, and accountability.

That's why apostles must be recognized, tested, and affirmed —not self-appointed. Their authority comes from Christ, but it must also be received by the Church (2 Corinthians 10:8, 1 Thessalonians 2:6).

Apostolic Foundations Are Relational

In God's government, relationships matter more than titles. Apostolic order flows through covenant, not control. Paul didn't just visit churches with his "apostolic credentials." He referred to the churches as "my children," "my joy and crown," and "those whom I have begotten through the gospel." Apostolic order always comes with apostolic love. In fact, wherever you find true apostolic government, you'll also find:

- Spiritual fathers and mothers
- Healthy family environments
- Disciples being raised, not just entertained
- Truth spoken in love—even when it's uncomfortable
- Sons and daughters taking ownership and maturing in their callings

When apostles walk as fathers, and churches embrace that covering, revival finds a wineskin. God's presence and purpose dwell where His pattern is honored.

Why Apostolic Order Matters for Every Believer

You might be thinking, "I'm not a leader—why does this matter to me?" Because how a house is built affects everyone living in it. If a house has poor structure, the family suffers—whether through leaks, cracks, or safety issues. In the same way, when churches lack apostolic order, the people suffer. There's confusion, lack of growth, or spiritual vulnerability. But when a church is built on apostolic foundations:

- Truth is preached without compromise
- Discipleship is intentional, not accidental
- Leaders are held accountable in love
- Spiritual gifts flourish in healthy ways
- The next generation is equipped, not just entertained

Apostolic order isn't just for leadership teams—it's for the whole Body. It's for your growth, protection, and empowerment. It's how Jesus ensures His people are shepherded well and launched into destiny.

In Summary

- Apostles are master builders who lay the foundation of Christ in churches and leaders.
- Apostolic authority aligns and corrects, bringing divine order to the Body.
- There is a vital difference between spiritual gifting and governmental grace.
- Apostolic order flows through relationship, fatherhood, and humility—not titles.
- Every believer benefits from apostolic order because it creates a healthy, fruitful environment for spiritual growth.

Activation Prayer

Father, thank You that Jesus Christ is the Chief Cornerstone and that You build Your Church on a strong foundation. Thank You for raising up apostles as wise master-builders who align the Body with Heaven's blueprint. Lord, I submit my heart to Your divine order. Remove any cracks of independence, confusion, or rebellion in me, and lay in their place the foundation of truth, love, and alignment with Christ. Teach me to recognize the difference between gifting and true authority, and help me to honor those You have graced with apostolic leadership. Holy Spirit, build me into a living stone, rightly connected, so that I can grow strong, stable, and fruitful. Let my life reflect the order of Heaven and contribute to a healthy family where Your presence can dwell richly. In Jesus' name, Amen.

Discussion Questions

1. Paul called himself a "skilled master builder" (1 Cor. 3:10). How does the picture of apostles as architects change the way we think about their role in shaping churches, leaders, and culture?

2. This chapter stresses the difference between having a spiritual gift and carrying governmental grace. Why is it important not to confuse the two, and what dangers can come when gifting is elevated without accountability?

3. Apostolic order doesn't just affect leaders—it impacts every believer. How have you personally experienced the fruit (or the lack) of apostolic covering and order in a church setting?

7

SPIRITUAL COVERING AND AUTHORITY

PROTECTED TO FLOURISH

I n every household, covering is about protection. A roof doesn't restrict—it shields. A parent doesn't control—they guard, guide, and nurture. And in God's house, spiritual covering is no different. It is not about domination or religious hierarchy—it is about the Father's heart for His family.

God's government is always relational. From Genesis to Revelation, He reveals Himself not just as a King or Judge, but as a Father. And He governs His house not only through structure and order, but through relationships of honor, submission, and mutual love. The principle of spiritual covering flows from this heart.

Covering is not a man-made idea. It is a Kingdom reality rooted in the very nature of God's family. In this chapter, we'll uncover what spiritual covering truly is, how it protects and empowers, and how God's people can walk in submission without losing their identity or voice.

Covering Is Protection, Not Control

Some hear the word "authority" and immediately think of abuse, control, manipulation, or trauma. Sadly, many believers have experienced church leadership that operated in fear, pride, or ambition rather than in the heart of a shepherd. But that is not God's design.

In Scripture, authority is never meant to suppress—it's meant to protect and serve:

- Jesus said the greatest leaders are those who serve (Matthew 20:25–28).
- Paul told the Corinthians he had authority "for building you up, not tearing you down" (2 Corinthians 10:8).
- Shepherds are warned not to "lord it over the flock," but to lead by example (1 Peter 5:3).

True spiritual covering doesn't suffocate—it creates safety. It builds a roof over the house of God that keeps out the storms, guards from predators, and gives sons and daughters a place to grow. Apostolic and pastoral leaders are not called to be controlling figures, but protective fathers and mothers. When they function rightly, spiritual covering becomes a gift, not a burden.

What Is Spiritual Covering?

Spiritual covering is the divine order of relational authority that God establishes in His Church for the purpose of:

- Protection from deception, isolation, and spiritual warfare
- Accountability for character, decisions, and doctrine
- Growth into maturity, fruitfulness, and calling
- Alignment with Heaven's blueprint and the broader Body of Christ

Covering isn't just about who you are "under." It's about who is watching over your soul, walking with you, and willing to speak truth to you even when it's uncomfortable.

"Obey your leaders and submit to them, for they are keeping watch over your souls, as those who will have to give an account." — *Hebrews 13:17 ESV*

This doesn't mean blind obedience or spiritual dictatorship. It means honoring those who carry the weight of spiritual responsibility and embracing the gift of correction, counsel, and care.

Accountability Is for Everyone—Leaders and Members

Accountability isn't just for church members—it's for every person in the family, including the leaders. One of the signs of a healthy church is that no one is above correction. Apostolic covering means that even elders and pastors are submitted—first to Christ, then to other leaders in relationship. Paul held Peter accountable publicly when he began acting hypocritically in Galatians 2.

Timothy was instructed to not entertain accusations against elders without witnesses, but also to rebuke those who persist in sin. In a family, everyone has a voice—but not everyone has the same authority. That's not inequality; it's order. And in that order, everyone is accountable to someone. Without accountability:

- Leaders drift into pride or isolation
- Members slip into hidden sin or rebellion
- Relationships fracture through offense or secrecy
- Vision becomes vulnerable to division

But with covering and accountability, the church becomes a

place of safety, healing, and restoration—not shame or punishment.

The Spirit of Sons and Fathers

The spirit of this chapter is not institutional—it's relational. God governs His Church like a Father with sons and daughters. And He raises leaders to operate with that same heart.

"Though you have countless guides in Christ, you do not have many fathers. For I became your father in Christ Jesus through the gospel."
— *1 Corinthians 4:15 ESV*

There's a difference between spiritual babysitters and spiritual parents. Fathers and mothers carry responsibility, consistency, and love. They correct not to punish, but to restore. They cover not to control, but to shield. They lead not to be followed blindly, but to raise up sons and daughters who surpass them in every way. Likewise, spiritual sons and daughters carry a posture of:

- Honor for those who have gone before them
- Submission to wise counsel and direction
- Loyalty to the vision and values of the house
- Teachability and humility in their growth

This culture of honor and submission does not silence individuality—it frees it. It gives every believer room to grow, to be seen, and to flourish in the timing and wisdom of God.

Submission Is Strength, Not Weakness

In the world, submission is often viewed as a loss of power. But in the Kingdom, submission is the secret to authority. Even Jesus, the Son of God, walked in complete submission to the Father (John 5:19; Philippians 2:8). And because of that, He carried all authority in Heaven and Earth (Matthew 28:18). Submission in the Church doesn't mean mindless compliance—it means:

- Choosing to trust the process God placed you in
- Welcoming wise input before major decisions
- Staying in alignment when offense or impatience tempts you to withdraw
- Embracing spiritual family even when it's messy

When submission is mutual, relational, and Spirit-led, it becomes a foundation for favor, longevity, and fruitfulness.

How to Know You're Under Spiritual Covering

You're not truly "covered" just because you attend a church. Covering is a relational reality more than a positional one. Ask yourself:

- Do I have leaders who know me, speak into my life, and can correct me if needed?
- Do I regularly receive spiritual counsel and respond with humility?
- Do I feel safe enough to share my weaknesses and strong enough to accept truth?
- Do I align with the house's vision and remain submitted even when I disagree?

If the answer is yes, you are likely experiencing the gift of covering. And it will guard you more than you even realize. If not, don't be discouraged—seek alignment. Ask the Lord where He wants to plant you, who He wants you to walk with, and how you can grow into sonship with joy.

In Summary

- Spiritual covering is God's gift of protection, not a tool of control.
- Accountability creates a healthy culture for both leaders and members.
- Sons and fathers reflect God's heart for government through love and responsibility.
- Submission is strength—it positions us to walk in authority and favor.
- Every believer needs a place of covering to grow, be corrected, and be launched into their calling.

Activation Prayer

Father, thank You that Your government is relational, flowing from Your heart as a loving Father. Thank You for spiritual covering— not as control, but as protection, guidance, and nurture. I receive covering as a gift, not a burden. Lord, heal any wounds in me from unhealthy authority or misuse of leadership. Teach me to discern the difference between control and true fatherly care. Give me humility to submit where You've placed me, and courage to honor the leaders who watch over my soul. Holy Spirit, form in me the spirit of a son —a heart that honors, listens, and grows. And if You call me to cover others, help me to lead as a servant, not a lord; as a parent, not a dictator. May my life reflect the heart of Jesus, who submitted fully to the Father and carried all authority. In His name, Amen.

Discussion Questions

1 . This chapter compares a roof to spiritual covering— shielding, not restricting. How has your view of authority been shaped by past experiences, and how does Scripture redefine it as protection?

2 . Paul said, *"You have countless guides, but not many fathers"* (1 Corinthians 4:15). What is the difference between spiritual babysitters and spiritual parents, and why does the Church need true fathers and mothers today?

3 . In the Kingdom, submission is not weakness but the pathway to authority. How does Jesus' example of submission to the Father change the way you think about trusting and aligning with spiritual leaders?

8

APPOINTING AND COMMISSIONING LEADERS
THE WAY OF RECOGNITION AND RELEASE

G od does not promote people the way man does. In the Kingdom, leadership isn't seized—it's received. It isn't earned by striving—it's entrusted through faithfulness. The process of appointing and commissioning leaders in the Church is both sacred and strategic. It is how the Father entrusts His house to proven sons and daughters who carry His heart.

Throughout Scripture, we see that no one sends themselves. Leaders are recognized, affirmed, and released by those in authority, through prayer, discernment, and often, the laying on of hands. In this chapter, we'll walk through the biblical pattern for how elders, deacons, and bishops are chosen and commissioned—so that every member of the Church can recognize when a leader is truly sent by God.

Leaders Are Appointed, Not Self-Declared

There is a significant difference between aspiring to ministry and being appointed by God. While it's honorable to desire to serve the Church, the authority to govern, shepherd, and oversee others must come through recognition, confirmation, and relational commissioning.

"No one takes this honor upon himself, but he receives it when called by God, just as Aaron was." — Hebrews 5:4 NIV

In the New Testament, leaders were always appointed by other leaders. They were not self-promoted, elected by popularity, or chosen by natural gifting alone. They were raised up in relationship, tested in character, and sent with covering.

In Acts 14:23, Paul and Barnabas appointed elders in every church with prayer and fasting. In Acts 6, the apostles had the congregation select qualified men to serve as deacons, and then they laid hands on them. In 1 Timothy 5:22, Paul warns, "Do not be hasty in the laying on of hands," because commissioning is serious business.

The Role of the Apostolic in Appointing

Apostolic leaders carry the fathering and foundational authority to recognize grace and establish government. While every church community has a part to play, it is often apostles who carry the discernment and governmental anointing to affirm callings and release authority. Apostles don't simply look for charisma or talent—they look for:

- Fruitfulness over time
- Submission to covering
- Maturity in doctrine and lifestyle
- Servanthood before visibility

Just like Paul recognized Timothy's call and laid hands on him (2 Tim. 1:6), so apostolic leaders today are called to see the grace on others and activate it through commissioning.

The Process of Appointment

Though processes may vary slightly by context, Scripture gives us a consistent pattern for appointing leaders:

1. Observation and Recognition

Leaders are first seen before they are sent. Their faithfulness, fruit, and humility are visible to those around them.

"Let them also be tested first; then let them serve as deacons if they prove themselves blameless." — 1 Timothy 3:10 ESV

This period of observation protects the house from premature elevation and allows time for character to mature.

2. Affirmation by Leadership

Once someone has been tested and proven, existing leaders affirm the grace and calling on their life. This often includes apostolic or elder discernment as well as prophetic confirmation. Paul told Timothy not to neglect the gift he received when "the council of elders laid their hands on you" (1 Tim. 4:14).

3. Laying on of Hands and Commissioning

This is the moment of public recognition and spiritual impartation. The laying on of hands is not a ritual—it is a sacred transference of responsibility and grace. Through this act, the person being commissioned receives:

- Affirmation of their identity and call
- Impartation of spiritual authority
- Covering from the house and leadership
- Responsibility to steward the flock and their own life

Who Gets Appointed and Why

Each role in God's house—elders, deacons, and bishops—requires different graces but the same character. While titles differ, the qualifications are consistent:

- Above reproach
- Husband of one wife (faithful in covenant)
- Sober-minded, self-controlled, and disciplined
- Hospitable and able to teach (for elders)
- Not greedy or violent, but gentle and upright
- Good reputation with outsiders
- Proven in family life (1 Tim. 3; Titus 1)

These are not personality traits—they are signs of maturity, reliability, and trustworthiness. A deacon must first be a servant. An elder must first be a shepherd. A bishop must first be a father. None of these are rewards—they are assignments.

The Role of the Prophetic

While apostolic leaders often appoint and commission, the prophetic voice confirms. In Acts 13:2, it was during a time of prayer and fasting that the HolySpirit said, "Set apart for me Barnabas and Saul..." This prophetic directive launched Paul's apostolic ministry. When commissioning leaders:

- The prophetic brings clarity on timing and assignment
- The prophetic speaks to destiny and encouragement
- The prophetic works in harmony with apostolic authority, not outside of it

A healthy church honors both apostolic government and prophetic insight—structure and Spirit.

Commissioning as Sending

To be commissioned is not just to be recognized—it is to be sent. The word "apostle" literally means "sent one." And all leadership in the Church flows from this sending grace. You are not just appointed to a role—you are sent on a mission. Whether as:

- A deacon managing the practical needs of the house,
- An elder shepherding souls and teaching the Word,
- A bishop overseeing leaders and guarding doctrine,

You are commissioned to serve, protect, equip, and build. This is why covering and commissioning must be relational—not transactional. God doesn't just hand out titles. He entrusts sons and daughters with His people.

How Members Can Respond

If you are not yet a leader in your church, you still have a role to play. As you watch others be appointed and commissioned, here's how you can walk in honor and alignment:

- Celebrate the grace on others' lives, even if you don't yet understand it
- Trust your leaders to hear God as they affirm and appoint
- Serve faithfully and with joy—your time of recognition will come
- Pray for those who lead, that they walk in purity and strength

Every healthy church has a process for releasing leaders—not out of politics or preference, but out of Kingdom purpose. When this is done rightly, the Church multiplies—not just in numbers, but in strength.

In Summary

- Leaders in the Church are appointed, not self-promoted
- Apostolic and elder leadership recognize, test, and commission
- The process includes observation, affirmation, and laying on of hands
- Every leader must meet biblical qualifications of character and maturity
- The prophetic plays a role in confirming assignments
- Commissioning is not about position—it's about Kingdom mission
- Members grow by walking in honor, submission, and service

Activation Prayer

Father, thank You that leadership in Your Kingdom is not seized but entrusted. Thank You for appointing and sending leaders who carry Your heart, Your character, and Your mission. I honor the sacred process of recognition, affirmation, and commissioning. Lord, protect my heart from striving, ambition, or self-promotion. Teach me to serve faithfully, to walk in humility, and to trust Your timing for my life. Help me to celebrate the grace You place on others, even as I wait for my own season of recognition. Holy Spirit, make me sensitive to the order of Your house. Whether You call me to lead or to serve, let me do it with purity, accountability, and love. Position me in relationships of covering, so that I may be corrected, equipped, and released in Your way, not mine. In Jesus' name, Amen.

Discussion Questions

1 . Hebrews 5:4 says no one takes spiritual honor for themselves, but receives it when called by God. How does this challenge the way our culture often views leadership, ambition, and promotion?

2 . This chapter describes three stages: observation, affirmation, and laying on of hands. Why is each stage important, and what dangers arise if any of these steps are rushed or skipped?

3 . If you are not yet in leadership, how can you still participate in the process of commissioning? What practical ways can you pray for, support, and honor leaders who are being recognized and sent?

9

GOVERNMENT THAT PRODUCES GROWTH

W hen many people hear the word government, their minds race to images of restriction, control, or power struggles. But in God's Kingdom, government doesn't crush—it cultivates. It doesn't restrict—it releases. The divine design of Church government is meant to produce growth, not prevent it. It is meant to multiply sons and daughters, not micromanage them. When God's order is honored, it becomes a greenhouse for spiritual flourishing.

God's Government Equips, Not Dominates (Ephesians 4:11–13)

The foundation for all church government is found in Ephesians 4:11–13, where Christ gives five kinds of leaders—apostles, prophets, evangelists, pastors, and teachers—"to equip the saints for the work of ministry, for building up the body of Christ."

This means government in the Church is not about hierarchy or institutional control. It's about helping every member become who they were created to be. The goal is equipping, not elevating a few leaders. True authority in the Body of Christ always exists to serve the growth and maturity of the Body.

Jesus set the tone for this kind of leadership when He said, "Whoever wants to be great among you must be your servant" (Matt. 20:26). Kingdom government is always servant-hearted and others-focused. It equips by training, instructing, correcting, encouraging, and releasing—not by lording over or manipulating.

Healthy church government raises up mature sons and daughters who know how to hear God, obey Him, and serve others—not just passive attendees. And it gives them a place to function in the Body, not just consume from it.

Unity Through Order Produces Supernatural Fruit (Psalm 133)

Psalm 133 is a short chapter, but its impact is huge: "Behold, how good and pleasant it is when brothers dwell together in unity... For there the Lord has commanded the blessing, life forevermore."

This unity is not uniformity—it's alignment. It's a spiritual oneness under a shared government, shared vision, and shared values. Just like a physical body cannot function properly if the joints are out of place, a spiritual body cannot flourish without proper order.

Unity in the Church doesn't come from everyone thinking the same—it comes from everyone being in their proper place. A foot doesn't need to become a hand to belong. A deacon doesn't need to be an elder to be honored. When every part of the body embraces their God-given role and submits to God's order, the result is harmony—and in that place, God commands a blessing. The fruit of unity through godly government includes:

- Peace in the house
- Growth among believers
- Protection from spiritual attack
- The manifest presence of God
- Multiplication and sending

The Church becomes like a healthy family where everyone knows who they are, what they carry, and how they fit.

Spiritual Alignment Brings Protection

One of the most overlooked blessings of biblical government is protection. In a world where spiritual warfare is real, the structure of the Church is meant to be a covering, not a cage. Just as a roof covers a home, spiritual authority covers the Body. Elders, deacons, and bishops—when functioning properly—create a canopy of safety where wolves are kept out, deception is exposed, and sin is lovingly confronted.

Alignment to God's order isn't legalism—it's wisdom. Just as a soldier in battle doesn't act alone but functions under chain of command for protection and effectiveness, so the saints of God walk under covering for their strength and safety. Spiritual alignment means:

- Submitting to authority without losing personal responsibility
- Trusting that God has placed you in a body for your good
- Being corrected when needed—and growing from it
- Walking in grace that flows from the head down (see Psalm 133 again)

Those who resist authority often live vulnerable, spiritually isolated lives. But those who honor God's order walk in supernatural peace and strength.

Alignment Leads to Multiplication and Maturity

Churches that are governed biblically don't just grow in numbers—they grow in depth. Maturity is the fruit of order. In Acts 6, when the apostles appointed deacons to help with food distribution, the result was that "the word of God continued to increase, and the number of the disciples multiplied greatly" (Acts 6:7). Why? Because the right people were in the right place, doing the right things. Government released growth.

Likewise, in Exodus 18, Moses learned that if he didn't delegate responsibility, he would wear out the people. But when he appointed leaders of thousands, hundreds, fifties, and tens, the people were better served—and Moses could focus on hearing from God. Churches that do not have healthy government often plateau or burn out. But churches that embrace God's blueprint grow deep and wide:

- Deep in character, maturity, and spiritual fruit
- Wide in reach, impact, and sending

And not just the church grows—the people grow. Saints become ministers. Children become spiritual mothers and fathers. Gifts are discovered and stewarded. Lives flourish under God's divine rhythm.

A Family That Grows Together

Ultimately, God's government looks like a family. Elders are spiritual fathers, deacons are trustworthy siblings, bishops are seasoned overseers, and apostles are master-builders who see the big picture. And the saints are the sons and daughters being equipped to inherit the family business—the Kingdom of God.

God is not raising up spectators. He is raising up sons and daughters. And He places them in a house, under covering, in alignment—not to limit them, but to launch them. When the Church walks in the rhythm of God's order, it becomes a place where people don't just attend—they ascend. They grow up into Christ. They grow together in love. And they multiply the Kingdom everywhere they go.

Activation Prayer

"Father, thank You for placing me in Your house. I choose to honor Your order and trust the covering You've placed over my life. Teach me to walk in unity, serve with joy, and grow in every season. Help me become a mature son or daughter who brings fruit and glory to Your name. Amen."

Reflection Questions

1 . What is your current view of spiritual authority? How does it align with Scripture?

2 . Have you ever experienced the blessing of covering and alignment in a church family?

3 . In what ways can you actively contribute to unity and order in your local church?

10

HANDLING CONFLICT, CORRECTION AND CHURCH DISCIPLINE

Conflict in the Church is inevitable—but chaos is not. Correction is necessary— but condemnation is not. Church discipline is biblical—but it must be rooted in love, not control. When God establishes government in His house, it is not to police people but to restore them. His leadership is always redemptive in purpose. A healthy understanding of how conflict and correction are handled within God's order brings security to the saints and protection to the church.

Conflict Is Normal—Division Is Not

Every family has conflict. Siblings fight. Parents disagree. Offense happens. But what makes a family strong is not the absence of conflict—it's how they respond to it. Jesus knew that disagreements and offenses would come. That's why He gave the Church a clear path for resolution in Matthew 18:15–17:

1. Go privately to the person.
2. If they don't listen, take one or two others.
3. If they still refuse, bring it before the church.

4. If they still resist, treat them as an outsider—not to shame them, but to clarify boundaries.

This process is rooted in grace, truth, and restoration. The goal is always healing, not punishment. In a healthy church governed by biblical order:

- People feel safe enough to confront in love.
- Leaders model humility and teachability.
- Offense is handled quickly and doesn't fester.
- Gossip and division are not tolerated.

Conflict becomes a catalyst for growth when handled under spiritual covering.

Correction Is an Act of Love

Hebrews 12:6 says, "The Lord disciplines the one He loves, and He chastens everyone He accepts as His son." In other words, correction is not rejection—it's proof that you belong. Spiritual leaders—elders, pastors, bishops—are called to correct when necessary.

This isn't because they're superior; it's because they are stewards of the flock. Ignoring sin or dysfunction would be neglect, not love. Correction includes:

- Speaking the truth in love (Eph. 4:15)
- Calling people back to their identity in Christ
- Exposing lies or sinful patterns with gentleness
- Holding people accountable with grace

The goal is never to tear down, but to build up. To bring clarity, not control. To restore alignment so the person can flourish again. Paul told Timothy, "Correct, rebuke and encourage—with great patience and careful instruction" (2 Tim. 4:2). That's the tone: patient, careful, instructive. Leaders correct because they care, not because they need control.

Church Discipline: Restoration Over Removal

When sin is unrepented, or a person becomes a danger to the health of the body, church discipline may be necessary. But it must always aim at restoration. Paul addressed this in 1 Corinthians 5. A man in the church was sleeping with his father's wife, and the church was tolerating it.

Paul said, "Hand this man over to Satan for the destruction of the flesh, so that his spirit may be saved on the day of the Lord." That sounds harsh—but it was redemptive. Paul was saying: create a boundary strong enough to wake him up so his soul can be restored.

Later, in 2 Corinthians 2, Paul writes that the man should now be forgiven and comforted, so he wouldn't be overwhelmed by excessive sorrow. Discipline worked—it led to repentance and healing. Church discipline may include:

- Temporarily removing someone from leadership or ministry roles
- Establishing boundaries for relational healing
- Encouraging a time of repentance, counseling, or deliverance
- Assigning spiritual oversight or mentorship during the process

All of this must be done with tears, not superiority. Discipline without love becomes abuse. But love without discipline becomes chaos. True Kingdom discipline restores the fallen, protects the innocent, and purifies the house.

The Role of Elders and Apostolic Oversight in Tough Situations

When serious conflict or correction is required, elders play a key role as spiritual fathers. Their job is not just to make decisions, but to shepherd hearts. They act as referees—not taking sides but seeking righteousness and reconciliation.

In cases of doctrinal error, rebellion, or division, apostolic oversight may be needed. Apostolic leaders carry a grace for setting things in order. They don't come to micromanage but to realign. Apostolic oversight helps:

- Maintain unity when tension arises
- Remove spiritual blind spots or pride
- Reaffirm what Scripture says when opinions clash
- Ensure that correction is both firm and fair

This is why churches need proper government—not just to run services, but to navigate storms. When government is in place, the house doesn't crumble under pressure.

Culture Matters: Truth with Grace, Honor with Boundaries

The way a church handles correction says a lot about its culture. Is it harsh and legalistic? Passive and permissive? Or loving, direct, and redemptive? A healthy church culture:

- Tells the truth even when it's hard
- Refuses gossip or accusation behind closed doors
- Calls out the gold in people even when correcting the dirt
- Builds a safe place for confession, healing, and new beginnings

This is why family language is so important in Kingdom government. In a true family:

- Sin is not hidden, but it's not exposed to shame either.
- Accountability is personal, not mechanical.
- Restoration is celebrated, not resented.

Correction is not for the purpose of exclusion but inclusion —to bring someone back into fellowship, wholeness, and purpose.

When the Church Governs Like Jesus

Jesus corrected His disciples often—but He never crushed them. He rebuked Peter, yet affirmed his calling. He confronted James and John's ambition, yet entrusted them with leadership. He challenged Thomas' doubt, yet invited him to touch His wounds. When the Church governs like Jesus:

- Conflict becomes a doorway to deeper trust.
- Correction becomes a mirror for growth.
- Discipline becomes a bridge to restoration.

And the result? A house that reflects the heart of the Father. A people who love the truth. A culture of safety, honor, and maturity.

Activation Prayer

"Lord, thank You for being a good Father who corrects in love. I choose to welcome Your discipline and embrace Your ways. Help me to grow in maturity, to walk humbly, and to honor the spiritual leaders You've placed in my life. Use me to create a culture of grace, truth, and restoration in Your house. Amen."

Reflection Questions:

1. How have you personally experienced correction in a healthy or unhealthy way in church life?

2. What does spiritual safety look like to you, and how can you help create it?

3. Why do you think God connects discipline with love?

11

FROM LOCAL CHURCH TO APOSTOLIC CENTER

In every generation, God raises up churches that are more than gathering places—they become sending bases. These are not merely pastoral flocks but apostolic hubs. While every church has a local expression, some are called to serve a regional or even global purpose. Understanding the difference between a local church and an apostolic center helps believers grasp the larger vision God has for advancing His Kingdom.

From Maintenance to Movement

Many churches operate in maintenance mode. Their focus is on keeping services running, caring for members, and maintaining internal programs. These are good and necessary things—but they are incomplete if they become the ceiling. Jesus never intended His Church to be stationary.

His final command was not to gather and hold meetings but to go and make disciples of all nations (Matt. 28:19). The Church was born as a movement, not a monument. An apostolic center is a church that has shifted from maintenance to movement. It sees itself as:

- A training ground for leaders
- A launching pad for ministry
- A governmental base for Kingdom influence
- A home where sons and daughters are matured and sent

The goal is not just to have a good Sunday service—but to send out equipped saints who will bring transformation in every sphere of society.

The Marks of an Apostolic Center

An apostolic center is not defined by its size or building—it's defined by its spiritual DNA and governmental structure. Here are some distinguishing marks:

1. Apostolic Leadership

- The church is led by an apostolic voice who carries vision, fathering grace, and regional responsibility.
- The lead elder or apostle equips others to lead, not just teaches people to follow.

2. Equipping and Sending

- The fivefold ministry is actively functioning to equip the saints.
- The church trains, activates, and commissions people into ministry—whether inside the church or in the marketplace.

3. Regional Influence

- Other leaders and churches look to the center for spiritual alignment, guidance, and support.

- There is a grace for governing—not controlling—other works through relationship and honor.

4. Prophetic and Strategic Vision

- The center functions with discernment of times and seasons (like the sons of Issachar).
- It operates with a blueprint mindset—not just what God is doing in the room, but what He's doing in the region.

5. Spiritual Sons and Daughters

- Discipleship goes beyond classes—it produces mature sons and daughters who reflect the culture and carry the vision.
- Honor, accountability, and spiritual inheritance flow freely.

6. Healthy Order and Government

- Elders, deacons, and bishops function biblically and in unity.
- Decision-making, correction, and commissioning happen under clear spiritual authority.

Training and Sending Leaders

The heart of an apostolic center is to multiply mature believers who carry the Kingdom wherever they go. This means:

- Raising up new elders and deacons
- Training pastors for church plants
- Equipping marketplace leaders to influence culture
- Sending missionaries into the nations

Ephesians 4 makes it clear: apostles, prophets, evangelists, pastors, and teachers are given not to perform ministry for the saints but to equip the saints to do the work of ministry. Apostolic centers take this seriously. They don't just gather—they graduate. People don't just sit—they serve. They don't just receive—they are released.

Planting Churches and Governing Territories

Just as Paul appointed elders in every city (Titus 1:5), apostolic centers often carry a regional assignment. This may involve:

- Planting churches in unreached or underdeveloped areas
- Forming apostolic networks of churches and leaders
- Hosting leadership gatherings for equipping and alignment
- Providing covering, counsel, and commissioning for ministries

This doesn't mean one church controls all others. True apostolic influence flows through relationship, honor, and spiritual authority, not hierarchy or domination. Apostolic centers govern through fathering, not franchising. They bless, cover, guide, and send—without micromanaging.

Apostles and Bishops Working Together

In an apostolic hub, bishops and apostles often function together. Bishops are mature leaders with oversight of elders and churches. Apostles may function similarly but carry unique grace for pioneering, foundation-laying, and Kingdom architecture. Where bishops tend to oversee existing works, apostles are often called to birth new ones. But in a healthy governmental model, they:

- Collaborate rather than compete
- Honor each other's grace
- Submit to mutual accountability
- Strengthen the body through unity

The goal isn't titles—it's Kingdom impact. Together, they guard doctrine, raise leaders, protect the flock, and extend the mission.

God's Vision: A Church That Sends

The book of Acts gives us a picture of this. Antioch became an apostolic center that:

- Trained and released Paul and Barnabas (Acts 13)
- Sent prophetic voices throughout the region
- Functioned as a hub for strategy, teaching, and correction

It wasn't the biggest or flashiest church—it was the healthiest and most obedient. And because of that, it became a launching point for global transformation. That's God's heart today. He wants churches to become more than gatherings. He wants them to become Governing Houses—centers of spiritual formation, alignment, and Kingdom sending.

What This Means for You

Even if you're not in leadership, this matters. Why? Because every believer has a role to play in an apostolic culture. Your maturity, your alignment, your service, and your yes to the Great Commission are vital. When the church is rightly governed:

- Your gift is recognized and cultivated
- Your calling is confirmed and commissioned

- You are covered, not controlled
- You are matured and mobilized

In an apostolic house, no one is a spectator. Everyone becomes part of God's building project.

Activation Prayer

"Father, thank You for building a Church that sends. I ask You to grow me into a mature son or daughter who carries Your Kingdom wherever I go. Align me with the house You've called me to, and help me serve, grow, and be released. Use me to be part of Your apostolic movement. In Jesus' name, amen."

Reflection Questions

1. Have you ever experienced a church that functions as a sending base? What stood out to you?

2. In what ways can you grow into someone who can be trained, trusted, and sent?

3. How does understanding apostolic centers change your view of what "church" is?

12

REFORMING THE WINESKIN

WHY THE CHURCH MUST RETURN TO BIBLICAL ORDER

Jesus said, "No one puts new wine into old wineskins" (Mark 2:22). This simple image reveals a profound truth: the outpouring of God's Spirit must be stewarded by the right structure. Just as wine requires a wineskin to hold it, revival, reformation, and Kingdom advancement require proper government to sustain them.

This chapter is a call to return—not to tradition or denominational control, but to biblical alignment. We must recover the New Testament blueprint if we want New Testament power. We must reform the wineskin if we want to carry the new wine.

When Man Builds What God Didn't Author

Much of what we've come to accept as "normal" church government is not found in Scripture. Instead of biblical models, many churches have adopted:

- Board-driven leadership based on business models
- Popular vote systems where carnal opinion overrules spiritual wisdom

- CEO-style pastors instead of fivefold teams
- Committee-run churches that limit the Spirit and frustrate leaders

These structures often emerge with good intentions—seeking checks and balances, financial integrity, or clarity. But when they replace God's divine pattern, they become man-made wineskins that cannot hold spiritual weight. They produce:

- Division and power struggles
- Leader burnout
- Shallow discipleship
- Resistance to revival

A biblical wineskin must be Kingdom-minded, not corporate-driven. It must flow from Heaven's order, not Earth's preferences.

Why the Church Needs Reformation in Government

Reformation is not rebellion—it's realignment. Throughout history, God has brought reform when His people drifted from His ways. The Protestant Reformation, the Azusa Street Revival, and modern apostolic movements were all fueled by a hunger to return to God's design. Today, God is reforming the wineskin of church government. Here's why:

1. The Church Must Be Governed by Revelation, Not Preference

- Jesus is the Head, and He sets leaders in place (1 Cor. 12:28).
- God calls, anoints, and confirms—not popular vote or politics.

2. The Saints Must Be Equipped, Not Entertained

- Fivefold government exists to equip the saints for ministry (Eph. 4:11–12).
- When churches become spectator-based, they lose power and purpose.

3. The Church Must Expand, Not Just Maintain

- Apostolic order produces fruit, multiplication, and movement.
- A pastoral-only model often keeps people safe but stagnant.

4. God's Glory Requires God's Order

- Unity and anointing flow where government is aligned (Psalm 133).
- God fills what reflects His pattern.

Signs of an Old Wineskin

To recognize the need for reform, we must know the signs of an old wineskin:

- Meetings without mission
- Committees without spiritual authority
- Control without covering
- Policies over presence
- No clear discipleship or leadership development pathway

Old wineskins focus on preserving comfort instead of pursuing transformation. They keep things "safe" at the expense of Kingdom progress. Jesus didn't come to patch the old. He came to give something new—but it requires a new container.

The Power of a Biblical Wineskin

A biblical wineskin is not just about the structure—it's about the spirit behind the structure. It reflects:

- Alignment with Christ as Head
- Fivefold ministry equipping every believer
- Elders and deacons functioning in biblical authority
- Spiritual covering, not control
- A culture of honor, submission, and maturity
- Apostolic vision that trains, sends, and governs with love

This wineskin doesn't restrict revival—it releases it. It doesn't hinder growth—it hosts it. When the wineskin is aligned, the new wine can flow freely—and be sustained.

Making the Shift: Reform in Action

Many churches today are in transition. They sense that what once worked no longer carries the weight of what God is doing now. They feel the tension between what is familiar and what is biblical. Here's how to begin making the shift:

1. Start with Revelation

- Let the Word of God reform your thinking.
- Study the early church's structure with fresh eyes.

2. Honor the Past, But Don't Idolize It

- Celebrate the faithfulness of what God has done.
- Be willing to move with the cloud—even if it means change.

3. Lead with Humility and Boldness

- If you're a leader, teach the Word with clarity and grace.
- If you're a member, support the shift with prayer and honor.

4. Build Slowly, but Build Right

- Don't rush the process—God builds line upon line.
- Prioritize culture and relationships over just roles and rules.

5. Recognize Who God Is Raising Up

- Apostles and prophets must be welcomed again—not as titles but as functions.
- Spiritual fathers and mothers are key to forming a family, not a factory.

The Wineskin of the Future is the Pattern of the Past

In reality, the "new" wineskin is the original one. We're not inventing something novel—we're recovering something ancient. The blueprint has always been there, in the Word. We are in a time where God is restoring the government of His house so that:

- The saints are equipped
- The leaders are aligned
- The regions are reached
- And the glory fills His temple

We must not settle for what is convenient. We must contend for what is Kingdom.

What This Means for You

You may wonder, "Why does this matter if I'm not a pastor or elder?" Because you are part of the house God is building. When the wineskin is right:

- You will be better pastored.
- You will grow into maturity.
- Your gifts will be recognized and activated.
- You'll experience deeper spiritual family and covering.
- You'll be launched into your calling—not stuck in a pew.

The government of the Church affects your growth, protection, and destiny. When Jesus reforms the wineskin, it's because He wants to pour more into you.

Activation Prayer

"Lord, I don't want to settle for the familiar—I want the fullness of Your pattern. Reform my heart, my mindset, and my house. Align me with Your design. Make me a wineskin that can carry the new wine. Let my church be a place where Your glory rests and Your people grow. In Jesus' name, amen."

Reflection Questions

1 . Have you seen man-made structures hinder spiritual growth in a church?

2 . What part of the biblical model resonates most with you?

3 . Are you willing to embrace the change God is calling His Church into?

CONCLUSION
CHRIST THE KING, HIS BODY IN ORDER

At the center of all government—whether in Heaven or on Earth—is a King. Not a system, a philosophy, or a board. A King. That King is Jesus. He is the Head of the Church, the Cornerstone of the House, the Bridegroom of the Bride, and the Chief Shepherd of the flock.

All government in the Church exists to reflect His Lordship, carry out His will, and equip His people to walk in His fullness. This book has not been about titles, positions, or religious hierarchy. It has been about order that brings life, structure that hosts glory, and leadership that reflects the nature of the Father.

The Church is a Body, Not a Business

We live in a time when the Church has often been treated like a company to be managed or a crowd to be entertained. But Scripture tells a very different story. The Church is:

- A body, where every part must be rightly connected (1 Corinthians 12)

- A family, with fathers and mothers, sons and daughters (Ephesians 3:14–15)
- A temple, built together for God's presence to dwell (Ephesians 2:19–22)
- A government, where Christ reigns through order and honor (Isaiah 9:6–7)

That's why how we govern matters. It's not about control—it's about Christ being seen and known through a Church that looks like Him.

When Christ is the Head, the Body Comes Alive

The reason for recovering biblical church government is not to restrict people but to release them. When Jesus is truly the Head:

- The fivefold ministry equips every saint.
- Elders shepherd and protect the flock with wisdom and love.
- Deacons meet the practical needs with excellence and faith.
- Bishops oversee the work with maturity and multiplied fruit.
- Apostolic fathers and mothers raise up sons and daughters.
- Disciples grow, flourish, and go.

A Church aligned with Heaven's government is a living organism—full of Spirit, truth, unity, and power.

We Are Becoming the House He Can Dwell In

Throughout the Bible, God's presence rests where His pattern is followed:

- Moses built the tabernacle "according to the pattern" and the glory came (Exodus 40:33–34).
- Solomon dedicated the temple "in order" and the fire fell (2 Chronicles 7:1–2).
- The early Church "continued steadfastly" in apostolic structure and multiplied daily (Acts 2:42–47).

God still desires a house where His name dwells. But He will not bless what He didn't build. He is calling His Church back to His blueprint, not for nostalgia—but for His glory to return in power.

You Have a Place in the House

This book has not only been written for pastors, elders, or leaders—but for every believer who is part of God's family. Because when the house is healthy, you thrive. When leaders lead rightly:

- You're covered, not controlled.
- You're equipped, not overlooked.
- You're released, not restricted.
- You're matured, not manipulated.

This is the kind of house Jesus is building. And you have a role to play:

- Learn to honor those God has placed over you.
- Be willing to grow into maturity and serve with faithfulness.
- Pray for your leaders and church family to walk in alignment.
- Embrace the protection, correction, and commissioning of true spiritual government.

God's house is not a place of religious duty—it's a place of Kingdom identity and destiny.

Let the Glory Fill the House Again

In Haggai 2:9, the Lord makes a stunning promise: "The glory of this latter house shall be greater than the former..." God desires to fill His Church with His glory—but that glory will rest on a house in order. A family walking in unity. A body under the Head. A people governed by Heaven's blueprint. Now is the time to build. Not with wood, hay, and stubble—but with wisdom, grace, and truth.

Now is the time to align. Not with traditions of men, but with the order of Christ. Now is the time to arise. Not as scattered sheep, but as a glorious ecclesia—governed by love, led by the Spirit, and rooted in the Word.

This is the Church that hell cannot prevail against.

This is the Church Jesus is coming back for.

This is the Church that governs God's house.

Final Declaration

Jesus, You are the Head. We submit to Your Lordship. We align with Your Word. We honor the leaders You have placed. We take our place in the body. We welcome Your glory. We will be the house You can dwell in. Let Your Kingdom come, and let Your will be done—in Your Church, as it is in Heaven.

ABOUT THE AUTHOR

Tom Cornell is the Senior Leader of SOZO Church in Washington state, founder of Walk in the Light International and SOZO Network. Tom is married to his beautiful wife Katy and lives in the Puget Sound area with her and their three kids. He has been in ministry pastoring and teaching the body of Christ since 2008.

He has a passion to see the body of Christ moving from people with an orphan mindset to that of sonship; equipping the body to do the work of Jesus resulting in seeing the Kingdom of God manifested here on earth.

www.ingramcontent.com/pod-product-compliance
Lightning Source LLC
Chambersburg PA
CBHW071236090426
42736CB00014B/3108